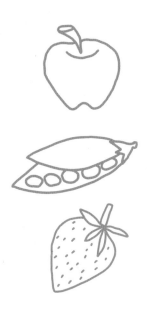

little cooks

authors
Erin & Tatum Quon

photographer
David Matheson

weldon**owen**

contents

about this book

Cooking with your kids is a fun activity the whole family can enjoy together. This collection of easy-to-prepare, family-friendly recipes encourages creativity in the kitchen and teaches everyone—adults and kids alike—how easy it is to prepare delicious, healthy dishes with fresh ingredients. In the pages that follow, you will find new twists on old favorites, such as French toast bites with blueberry sauce and inside-out apple crisp, as well as classics like chicken potpie and ice cream bonbons. Colorful photos of yummy food and ideas on how to make fun variations will grab your kids' attention and have them eager to help.

TATUM QUON

getting started

Our lives are a lot busier and it's hard to find the time to teach our kids basic cooking skills that will help them as they grow. With inspiring recipes and dishes the whole family will love to make and eat, this book will help you get started doing just that. Here are some tips for keeping things fun in the kitchen:

Choose a recipe Decide together what you want to make, then read through the recipe so there are no surprises.

Gather your ingredients Get out all of the ingredients and tools you'll need for making the recipe.

Prepare your ingredients Rinse and dry off fruits and vegetables before you use them. Handle delicate ingredients, like berries and tomatoes, gently. Give tough-skinned produce, like potatoes and carrots, a good scrub. It's also a good idea to measure everything out before you begin making the recipe.

Keep it safe Adults should always stay in the kitchen to lend a hand when needed. It's okay to ask questions as you work or to ask for help when needed.

Clean it up Clear off and clean a space that's big enough to cook comfortably. Clean up work surfaces and tools as you use them, and wash your hands with warm water and soap before you handle anything. Being neat as you cook makes cleanup easier and cooking more fun.

using the recipes

The recipes in this cookbook are intended for kids ages 4–8, to use with as much independence as seems right for their age and skill level. Only you, the parents, can gauge how much support you will need to give your children as they cook. Help your children by reviewing the recipe with them before they begin and going over any questions they may have. To make this process easier, we have designed the recipes to identify the steps that kids can do on their own. These are our suggestions only, not strict requirements.

for parents

Each recipe contains steps which are meant for you, the parent, to take the lead on, like using knives for chopping, stirring on a hot stovetop, and putting things in and pulling them out of the oven. However, you know your children's skill levels best, so have them help out as much or as little as you feel comfortable.

for kids

 Every recipe in this book includes call outs for kids. Just look for the chef's hat and the orange text, review the step with your parent, and get started. If you need help, just ask. It's always better to be safe!

rise & shine

There are few better ways to rouse your little sleepyheads from their slumber than the promise of breakfast made together. Pancakes the size of silver dollars. Crunchy homemade granola. Crisp cubes of cinnamon French toast ready for dipping. Morningtime goodies offer ample opportunity for even the smallest kids to accomplish much of the preparation themselves. Just pull a kitchen stool up to the counter and let the kids take charge.

breakfast pinwheels

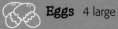

 Eggs 4 large

 Cheddar cheese
½ cup shredded

 Salt and pepper
Big pinch each

 Butter 2 tablespoons

**Whole wheat
tortillas** 2 (6-inch)

Ham 4 slices

Makes 2 servings

 In a bowl, whisk together the eggs and ¼ cup of the cheese. Season with salt and pepper.

In a sauté pan over medium heat, melt 1 tablespoon of the butter. Add the eggs and cook, stirring constantly with a spatula, until cooked through but still soft and moist, about 6 minutes. Remove from the heat, transfer to a bowl, and set aside.

 Lay the tortillas on a work surface. Scoop half of the scrambled eggs onto the top of each tortilla. Sprinkle the remaining ¼ cup of cheese on top of the eggs, dividing it evenly between the tortillas. Top each tortilla with 2 slices of the ham. Working from the edge closest to you, roll up each tortilla.

Cut each rolled tortilla into 3 pieces. Pierce each piece with a toothpick to secure and serve.

waffles with strawberry sauce

Preheat a waffle iron. Preheat the oven to 250°F.

Place the strawberries in a blender. Add the brown sugar, orange juice, and ¼ teaspoon vanilla. Blend until smooth. Set aside.

To make the waffles, in a large bowl, stir together the flour, granulated sugar, baking powder, and baking soda. In another bowl, whisk together the egg yolks, buttermilk, milk, butter, and remaining ¼ teaspoon vanilla. Pour the buttermilk mixture into the flour mixture and stir until blended.

In a bowl, beat the egg whites using an electric mixer on medium speed until soft peaks form. Using a rubber spatula, fold the beaten egg whites into the flour-buttermilk mixture just until combined.

Lightly grease the waffle iron and ladle in enough batter for 1 waffle. Close the lid of the iron and cook according to the manufacturer's directions. When the waffle is ready, transfer it to a rimmed baking sheet and keep warm in the oven. Repeat with the remaining batter, adding each finished waffle to the baking sheet without stacking the waffles.

Cut the waffles into sticks or wedges and serve them with the stawberry sauce for dipping.

Strawberries
2 cups, hulled

Brown sugar
2 tablespoons

Orange juice
2 tablespoons

Vanilla extract
½ teaspoon, divided

All-purpose flour
1½ cups

Granulated sugar
2 tablespoons

Baking powder
2 teaspoons

Baking soda
1 teaspoon

Large eggs 2, separated

Buttermilk 2 cups

Milk ¼ cup

Butter ¼ cup, melted

Makes 6–8 waffles

 Olive oil
2 tablespoons

 Small baking potatoes 2, peeled and diced

 Breakfast sausage
10 ounces, casings removed

 Large eggs 4

 Milk ¼ cup

 Grated Parmesan cheese ¼ cup

Makes 12 mini frittatas

little frittatas

Preheat the oven to 375°F.

Line a 12-cup mini-muffin pan with paper liners.

In a large frying pan over medium heat, warm the olive oil. Add the potatoes and sauté until they begin to soften, about 5 minutes. Crumble in the sausage meat and cook, stirring often, until golden brown, about 6 minutes. Remove from the heat and transfer to a bowl to cool slightly.

In a bowl, whisk together the eggs, milk, and cheese until blended. Stir in the cooled sausage and potatoes.

Scoop the mixture into the lined muffin cups, dividing it evenly.

Bake until firm and doubled in size, 10–15 minutes. Let cool slightly in the pan before serving.

french toast bites with blueberry sauce

 Blueberries 1 pint

 Maple syrup ¾ cup

 Sugar 2 tablespoons

 Ground cinnamon 1 teaspoon

 Large eggs 2

 Buttermilk ½ cup

 Milk ½ cup

 Vanilla extract 1 teaspoon

 Salt Pinch

 Country bread 6 thick slices, cut into 1-inch cubes

 Butter 2 tablespoons

Makes 4 servings

In a small saucepan over medium-low heat, combine the blueberries and maple syrup. Bring to a boil, stirring to prevent scorching, then remove from the heat and set aside to let cool.

 In a large bowl, stir together the sugar and cinnamon. Set aside.

 In a large shallow bowl, whisk together the eggs, buttermilk, milk, vanilla, and salt until blended. Place the bread cubes in the egg mixture and, using a large spoon, toss gently until the cubes are evenly coated and all the egg mixture has been absorbed.

In a large frying pan over medium heat, melt 1 tablespoon of the butter. Add half of the coated bread cubes and cook, turning often, until golden brown on all sides, about 5 minutes. Transfer the cubes to the bowl holding the cinnamon-sugar and toss to coat. Repeat with the remaining bread cubes and 1 tablespoon butter.

Divide the french toast bites into individual servings and sprinkle with the remaining cinnamon-sugar. Serve with the blueberry sauce.

Buttery and crisp on the outside, soft on the inside, French toast is perfect for many preparations. Try skewering it with fresh fruit or just sprinkling on some confectioners' sugar. Or, use a spoonful of your favorite jam as a filling between 2 slices, then cook the toast with the filling sealed inside.

more french toast ideas

Alphabet sandwiches Have ready a whole loaf of sliced sandwich bread. Soak and cook as directed. Spread jam between 2 slices of French toast, cut into letter shapes, and sprinkle with confectioners' sugar.

French toast skewers Give kids a handful of small skewers and bowls of French toast cubes and fresh fruit. Let them load up the skewers as they wish.

French toast soldiers Cut sandwich bread lengthwise into ½-inch-wide "soldiers." Soak and cook as directed. Sprinkle with confectioners' sugar and serve with warmed maple syrup for dipping.

 All-purpose flour
2 cups

 Cornmeal 1¼ cups

 Baking powder
2 teaspoons

 Baking soda
½ teaspoon

 Salt ¼ teaspoon

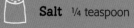 **Large eggs** 2

 Milk ⅔ cup

 Buttermilk ⅔ cup

 Butter 4 tablespoons,
melted

 Honey ¼ cup, plus
extra for serving

 Dried cranberries
1 cup

 Grated orange zest
1 teaspoon

Makes 24 muffins

crunchy cranberry muffin tops

Preheat the oven to 375°F. Line 2 rimmed baking sheets with parchment paper.

In a large bowl, stir together the flour, cornmeal, baking powder, baking soda, and salt. In a medium bowl, whisk together the eggs, milk, buttermilk, butter, and honey. Add the egg mixture to the flour mixture and stir until combined. Stir in the cranberries and orange zest and mix well.

Drop the batter by large spoonfuls onto the prepared baking sheets, placing them well apart.

Bake until golden, about 15 minutes. Transfer to a rack to cool for 4 minutes. Serve warm with honey.

yogurt sundaes

In a small bowl, stir together the yogurt, honey, and vanilla. Set aside.

In another small bowl, combine the strawberries, mango, blueberries, blackberries, and kiwifruit. Add the orange juice and stir gently until mixed.

Have ready 2 clear glass serving dishes. Spoon one-fourth of the yogurt mixture into each dish. Top each serving with one-fourth of the fruit mixture and then with one-fourth of the granola. Repeat the layers, ending with the granola. Serve at once, or cover and refrigerate for up to 3 hours before serving.

Plain yogurt 1 cup

 Honey 2 tablespoons

 Vanilla extract
¼ teaspoon

 Strawberries
¼ cup diced

 Mango ¼ cup diced

 Blueberries ¼ cup

 Blackberries ¼ cup

 Kiwifruit ¼ cup
diced

 Orange juice ¼ cup

 Granola ½ cup

Makes 2 sundaes

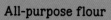

 All-purpose flour
1 cup

 Sugar 2 tablespoons

 Baking powder
2 teaspoons

 Baking soda
1 teaspoon

 Salt Pinch

 Milk 1 cup

 Large egg 1

 Unsalted butter
2 tablespoons, melted

 Vanilla extract
¼ teaspoon

 Canola oil
for greasing

 Bananas 2, sliced

Maple syrup
for serving

Makes 24–26
pancakes

silver-dollar pancake stacks

Preheat the oven to 250°F.

 In a large bowl, stir together the flour, sugar, baking powder, baking soda, and salt. In another bowl, whisk together the milk, egg, melted butter, and vanilla. Pour the milk mixture into the flour mixture and stir until no lumps are visible.

Heat a griddle pan or large frying pan, preferably nonstick, over medium heat. Lightly grease the pan with the canola oil. Using a tablespoon measure and working in batches, drop small rounds of batter onto the pan.

Cook the pancakes, turning them once with a spatula, until golden on both sides, about 3 minutes total. Transfer to a platter and keep warm in the oven. Repeat with the remaining batter, greasing the pan as needed.

 To serve, make stacks out of the pancakes. Use 3 pancakes for each stack and place banana slices in between each layer and on top. Drizzle with maple syrup and enjoy!

buttermilk biscuits with jam

All-purpose flour
2 cups, plus extra for sprinkling

Brown sugar
2 tablespoons, firmly packed

Baking powder
2 teaspoons

Baking soda
½ teaspoon

Salt Pinch

Butter 6 tablespoons cold, cut into small pieces, plus extra for serving

Buttermilk ¾ cup

Apricot jam ¼ cup

Makes about
12 biscuits

Preheat the oven to 450°F. Line a rimmed baking sheet with parchment paper.

In a large bowl, stir together the flour, brown sugar, baking powder, baking soda, and salt. Using your fingertips, rub the butter into the flour mixture until it looks like coarse crumbs, with some chunks the size of peas.

Add the buttermilk and stir until the dough starts to come together. Using your hands, press the dough into a rough ball, flatten into a disk, and place on a lightly floured work surface.

Using a rolling pin, roll out the dough, sprinkling the dough and work surface with flour as needed to prevent sticking, to an even thickness of about ½ inch. Using a 3-inch cookie or biscuit cutter, cut out as many biscuits as possible and place well apart on the prepared baking sheet. Gather up the scraps, press together, roll out, cut out more biscuits, and add them to the baking sheet.

Bake until golden, 12–15 minutes. Transfer to a rack and let cool briefly. Serve warm with butter and apricot jam.

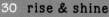

Savory or sweet, plain or dressed up, flaky buttermilk biscuits are a favorite breakfast staple. In fact, you're just as likely to find them served hot and fresh out of the oven alongside a generous helping of scrambled eggs and ham as you are spread thickly with butter and jam or drizzled with honey.

more biscuit ideas

Strawberry shortcake Top a biscuit half with an ample spoonful of cut fresh strawberries tossed with sugar, and top with a big dollop of whipped cream. Crown with the biscuit top to complete the dessert.

Ham & cheese sandwich A biscuit is perfect for a kid-sized sandwich. Fill it with slices of Cheddar cheese and ham, artfully folded for the ideal fit. Add mustard or mayonnaise to taste.

Peach "cobbler" Sprinkle cinnamon-sugar over peach halves and roast in a 450°F oven for 10 minutes. Serve atop biscuit halves for a fruity open-faced treat.

 Bacon 8 slices, diced

 Shredded sharp Cheddar cheese 1 cup

 Grated Parmesan cheese ¼ cup

 All-purpose flour 1 cup

 Salt 1 teaspoon

 Large eggs 2

 Milk 1¼ cups

Butter 2 tablespoons, melted, plus 1 tablespoon softened

Makes 12 popovers

cheesy bacon popovers

Preheat the oven to 450°F.

In a frying pan over medium heat, sauté the bacon until crisp, about 8 minutes. Transfer to paper towels to drain.

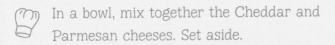 In a bowl, mix together the Cheddar and Parmesan cheeses. Set aside.

In a large bowl, stir together the flour and salt. In a medium bowl, whisk together the eggs, milk, and melted butter. Pour the milk mixture into the flour mixture and stir until smooth.

Grease a 12-cup muffin pan with the softened butter. Spoon about 1 tablespoon of the bacon and 1½ tablespoons of the cheese mixture into each cup of the prepared pan.

Ladle the egg mixture into the muffin cups, dividing it evenly. Bake for 15 minutes, then reduce the oven temperature to 350°F. Make sure you do not open the oven while the popovers are baking or they will fall! Continue baking until the popovers are puffed and golden, about 15 minutes longer. Transfer the popovers to a rack to cool briefly. Serve warm.

breakfast "BLT" triangles

 Bacon 6 slices

 Whole wheat bread
4 slices, toasted

 Butter 1 tablespoon

 Large eggs 2

 Plum (roma) tomato
1, sliced

 Salt and pepper
to taste

Makes 2 sandwiches

In a large frying pan over medium heat, cook the bacon, turning once, until crisp, about 8 minutes. Transfer to paper towels to drain briefly.

 Divide the bacon slices evenly between 2 slices of the toasted bread.

In a nonstick frying pan over medium heat, melt the butter. One at a time, crack the eggs on the countertop and add them to the pan. Reduce the heat slightly and cook, turning once, until the whites are crisp around the edges and the yolks are firm, about 6 minutes total. Using a spatula, place the eggs on top of the bacon.

 Top each egg with tomato slices. Sprinkle the tomatoes with salt and pepper, then place a second slice of toast on top of each stack to make 2 yummy sandwiches.

Cut each sandwich into triangle quarters and serve.

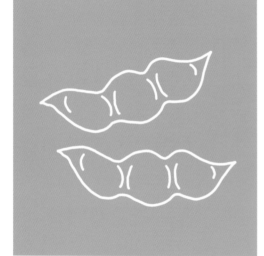

snacktime

When a quick fix is needed, or after the haze of a midmorning or afternoon nap, nothing revives more readily than a homemade, wholesome snack. Whether threading mozzarella and tomatoes on skewers, popping corn on the stovetop, or simply spreading peanut butter onto apple slices for fruit "pizzas," snacktime can provide nutritious and entertaining ideas for kids during an otherwise humdrum time of day.

Canola oil ⅓ cup

Popcorn kernels ½ cup

Salt 3 teaspoons

Confectioners' sugar ¼ cup

Grated Parmesan cheese 1 cup

Butter 3 tablespoons, melted

Makes 4 servings

sweet-n-salty popcorn bags

Pour the canola oil into the bottom of a large, heavy saucepan and heat over medium heat. Add the popcorn kernels, cover, and cook, shaking the pan often, until you start to hear popping. Continue to cook, shaking the pot continuously, until the popping slows to 3–5 seconds between pops. Remove from the heat and divide the popcorn evenly between 2 bowls.

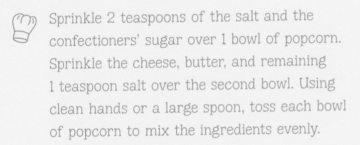 Sprinkle 2 teaspoons of the salt and the confectioners' sugar over 1 bowl of popcorn. Sprinkle the cheese, butter, and remaining 1 teaspoon salt over the second bowl. Using clean hands or a large spoon, toss each bowl of popcorn to mix the ingredients evenly.

Scoop the popcorn evenly into individual popcorn bags—sweet in one bag and cheesy in another—and serve right away.

pizza kabobs

 Have ready 12 short wooden skewers. Working with 1 skewer at a time, alternately thread 2 tomatoes, 2 basil leaves, and 2 mozzarella balls onto each skewer. Or, divide the ingredients among the skewers as you like.

 Place the skewers on a serving dish and drizzle with the olive oil. Sprinkle with salt and pepper to taste and serve.

 Cherry tomatoes
1 pint

 Small basil leaves
24

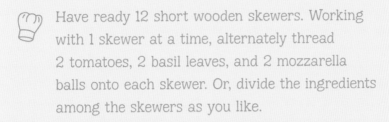 **Small mozzarella balls** 24

 Olive oil
2 tablespoons

 Salt and pepper
to taste

Makes 12 kabobs

There is something about the simple act of poking stuff onto a stick that can keep kids busy for hours. Give them a set of plain wooden skewers alongside bowls filled with pieces of fresh fruit or cubes of cheese and lunch meats, and the activity becomes filled with a sense of yummy purpose and healthy sensibility.

more kabob ideas

Mixed fruit Any fruit is a good option for skewers, although fresh, seasonal choices will offer the most flavor. Try chunks of mango, kiwifruit, watermelon, cantaloupe, honeydew, or pineapple.

Strawberry cake Pair fresh strawberries or pitted cherries with bite-size cubes of vanilla or chocolate pound cake or angel food cake for a little taste of something sweet in the afternoon.

Salami & Swiss If snacktime runs closer to mealtime, offer items with a bit more substance for skewering. Try cubes of salami and Swiss or ham and Cheddar.

Red and yellow cherry tomatoes
1 pint each

Olive oil
2 tablespoons

Salt 1 teaspoon

Sandwich bread
8 slices

Cheddar cheese
8 sandwich-sized slices

Butter 4 tablespoons

Makes 4 servings

grilled cheese sticks with tomato soup dip

Preheat the oven to 350°F.

 Spread out the tomatoes on a rimmed baking sheet. Drizzle with the olive oil and sprinkle with the salt. Using your hands, toss the tomatoes gently to coat evenly with the oil and salt.

Bake the tomatoes until they pop open, about 15 minutes. Remove from the oven, let cool for 5 minutes, and transfer to a blender.

 Pulse the tomatoes in the blender until smooth. Then, top 4 slices of bread with 2 slices of cheese each, and cover with the remaining 4 bread slices.

Pour the tomato purée through a fine-mesh sieve set over a small saucepan, discarding the contents of the sieve. Place the saucepan over low heat and heat until hot.

Meanwhile, in a large frying pan over medium heat, melt the butter. Add the sandwiches and cook, turning once, until golden brown on both sides and the cheese has melted, about 5 minutes total.

Pour the soup into 4 small bowls. Cut each sandwich into 4 "sticks." Serve alongside the soup for dipping.

apple–peanut butter pizzas

Golden Delicious or Granny Smith apples 2 large

Creamy peanut butter ¾ cup

Flaked coconut, dried cranberries, and granola
About ⅓ cup each

Makes 12–14 pizzas

Using an apple corer, core the apples. Cut each apple crosswise into 6 or 7 rounds.

 Using a small spreader, spread about 1 tablespoon of the peanut butter on each apple slice. Sprinkle the slices with the coconut, dried cranberries, and granola and serve.

 Chickpeas
1 can (15 ounces)

 Tahini 2 tablespoons

 Lemon juice
2 tablespoons

 Ground cumin
1½ teaspoons

 Salt 1 teaspoon

 Garlic 1 clove

 Olive oil ¼ cup

 **Whole wheat
tortillas** 2 (6-inch),
halved

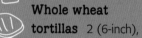 **English cucumber**
1, thinly sliced

 Carrots 2, shredded

Makes 4 cones

hummus & veggie cones

Pour the chickpeas into a sieve set over a small bowl. Measure out ¼ cup of the bean liquid and reserve; discard the remaining liquid.

 Place the chickpeas in a food processor or blender. Add the tahini, lemon juice, cumin, salt, garlic, and reserved chickpea liquid and blend until smooth. With the food processor or blender running, slowly drizzle in the olive oil and continue to blend until the mixture is very smooth. Set aside.

 Lay the tortilla halves on a cutting board. Spread each tortilla half with an equal amount of the hummus. Cover the hummus with cucumber slices. Sprinkle the carrots evenly over the cucumber. Starting at a corner, roll up each tortilla into a cone and serve.

orange-yogurt pops

Fresh orange juice
2 cups

Vanilla yogurt
1 cup

Makes 4 pops

In a large bowl, stir together the yogurt and juice. Pour the mixture into 4 molds of an ice-pop tray, dividing it equally.

Insert an ice-pop holder or wooden ice-pop stick into each mold. Freeze for at least 8 hours or up to overnight.

When ready to serve, run the molds under warm water for a few seconds to release the pops.

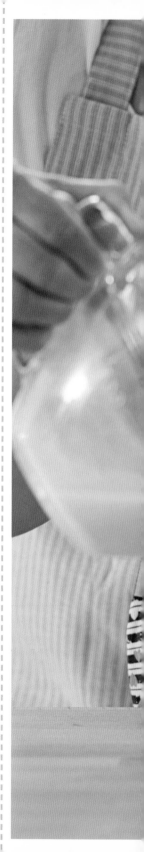

When the afternoon doldrums strike, few snacks revive kids as quickly as these cool, fruity pops. With only 2 ingredients, this recipe is a cinch for kids to master. They will find it easy to substitute their favorite flavors for the original, and to mix and blend different fruit flavors and colors for their own unique pops!

more yogurt pop ideas

Fruit juice slices Pour blended yogurt into loaf pans before freezing, then unmold, slice, and eat with a fork. Or, leave the fruit juice out and try layering the loaf pans with different flavors of yogurt.

Multiflavored pops Most kids appreciate a choice when it comes to fruit flavors. Try adding grape, cherry, or tropical fruit juice as an alternative to the orange.

Fruit cups Scatter a spoonful of fresh berries over the bottom of a ramekin. Add a complimentary flavor of blended yogurt and freeze. Before serving, dip the bottom of the ramekin in warm water, then unmold.

granola bites

 Butter 2 tablespoons, plus extra, softened for greasing

 Shredded coconut 1 cup

 Dried cherries 1 cup

 Dried blueberries ½ cup

 Old-fashioned rolled oats 2 cups

 Whole almonds 1 cup

 Shelled sunflower seeds 1 cup

 Wheat germ 1 cup

 Brown sugar 1 cup, firmly packed

 Honey ½ cup

 Vanilla extract 1 teaspoon

 Ground cinnamon 1 teaspoon

Makes about 16 squares

Preheat the oven to 350°F.

 Grease a 9-inch square pan with the softened butter. In a large bowl, combine the coconut, cherries, and blueberries; set aside. On a rimmed baking sheet, combine the oats, almonds, sunflower seeds, and wheat germ.

Bake the oat mixture until toasted and fragrant, 5–10 minutes. Remove from the oven. Add the hot oat mixture to the fruit-coconut mixture and stir until combined.

In a saucepan over medium heat, melt the butter. Add the brown sugar, honey, vanilla, and cinnamon and stir until the sugar dissolves, about 5 minutes. Bring to a boil, then remove from the heat and pour over the fruit-oat mixture.

 Using a large spoon, gently stir together all the ingredients until well combined. Scoop the mixture into the prepared pan. Using your hands, firmly press the mixture into the pan, making a compact, even layer. The mixture will be sticky!

Let set in the pan for 10 minutes. Invert the pan onto a cutting board and lift off the pan. Cut into squares and serve.

edamame snack

 In a bowl, stir together the soy sauce, sesame seeds, and sugar.

Bring a large pot of water to a boil over high heat. Add the edamame and boil for 5 minutes. Drain.

 Add the beans to the soy sauce mixture. Using clean hands or a large spoon, toss gently to coat the beans with the sauce.

 To eat the edamame, peel away the pod and pop the beans into your mouth! Serve warm or at room temperature.

Soy sauce
2 tablespoons

Toasted sesame seeds
2 teaspoons

Sugar ¼ teaspoon

**Frozen edamame
in their pods**
10-ounce bag, thawed

Makes 4 servings

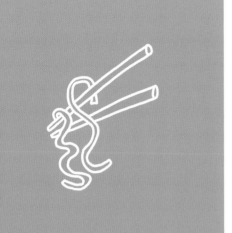

supper

Kids won't need much encouragement to eat a nutritious dinner when they help make the supper themselves. In a kid's kitchen, pride of ownership can do more to inspire a big appetite than any amount of bargaining. Focus on menu items that include hands-on fun like ravioli, meatballs, tacos, and pizza. Make it interesting by letting them add all the ingredients themselves and vary them according to their own tastes.

 Large sweet potatoes 2, cut lengthwise into sticks

 Olive oil 2 tablespoons, plus extra for greasing

 Salt and ground pepper to taste

 Ground beef ¾ pound

 Cheddar cheese 2 slices, halved

 Small dinner rolls 4, split

 Dill pickle slices, ketchup, and mustard for serving

Makes 4 mini burgers

mini burgers with sweet potato fries

Preheat the oven to 400°F.

 Spread out the potato sticks on a rimmed baking sheet. Drizzle with the olive oil and sprinkle with salt and pepper. Using clean hands or a spatula, toss to coat evenly.

Bake until until golden and crisp, 20–25 minutes. Remove from the oven and keep warm.

 Meanwhile, divide the meat into 4 equal patties, each about ½ inch thick.

About 10 minutes before the fries are ready, using a basting brush, brush a stovetop grill pan or a cast iron frying pan with oil and place over medium-high heat. When the pan is hot, add the patties and cook, turning once, until browned on both sides, about 6 minutes total for medium. Top each burger with a piece of cheese during the final minute of cooking.

 Put each roll, cut sides up, on a serving plate. Place a burger on the bottom half of each roll. Accompany the burgers with pickle slices, ketchup, and mustard. Serve with the sweet potato fries alongside.

BLT salad

Preheat the oven to 400°F.

Spread out the bacon pieces on a rimmed baking sheet. Spread out the baguette cubes on a second rimmed baking sheet. Drizzle the olive oil over the baguette cubes. Using clean hands, toss the cubes to coat them evenly.

Put both baking sheets in the oven. Bake the baguette cubes until golden brown, about 10 minutes. Bake the bacon pieces until crisp, about 15 minutes.

When the baguette cubes are ready, remove them from the oven and let them cool. Then, when the bacon pieces are ready, remove them as well and transfer to paper towels to drain and cool.

To make the dressing, in a blender, combine the sour cream, lemon juice, Parmesan cheese, salt, and garlic. Blend until smooth.

In a large salad bowl, combine the lettuce, tomatoes, bacon, and baguette croutons. Drizzle with the dressing, toss to mix, and serve.

Bacon 8 slices, cut into bite-sized pieces

 Baguette 1, cut into bite-sized cubes

 Olive oil 2 tablespoons

 Sour cream ½ cup

 Lemon juice 2 tablespoons

 Grated Parmesan cheese 2 tablespoons

 Salt 1 teaspoon

 Garlic 1 clove, chopped

 Romaine lettuce 1 head, chopped

 Red and yellow cherry tomatoes 1 mixed pint, halved

Makes 4 servings

for the dough

 Lukewarm water
1¼ cups

 Active dry yeast
1 package (2½ teaspoons)

 Sugar 1 tablespoon

 All-purpose flour
3 cups, plus extra for
sprinkling

 Salt 1 tablespoon

 Olive oil 2 tablespoons,
plus extra for the bowl

for the toppings

 Jarred tomato sauce
15-ounce jar

 **Fresh mozzarella
cheese** 16 ounces, sliced

 **Sliced salami,
mushrooms, bell
peppers, and olives,
and basil leaves**

Makes 4 pizzas

pizza party

Preheat the oven to 500°F. To make the dough, pour the water into the bowl of a stand mixer, sprinkle with the yeast and sugar, and let stand until foamy, about 5 minutes. Add the flour, salt, and olive oil and beat on low speed until a rough, shaggy dough forms, about 5 minutes.

 Sprinkle a work surface with a little flour and dump the dough onto the surface. Knead with your hands until the dough is smooth and not sticky, about 5 minutes. Shape the dough into a ball. Oil a bowl with olive oil, put the dough in the bowl, and turn it to coat it with the oil. Cover the bowl with a kitchen towel. Let the dough rise until doubled in size, about 1 hour.

 Punch down the dough. Divide it into 4 fist-sized balls. Sprinkle a baking sheet with flour, place the balls on it, and cover with a kitchen towel. Let rise until doubled in size, about 30 minutes. Sprinkle the work surface with flour. Press each ball to deflate, then flatten and stretch it into a 10-inch round. Transfer the rounds to 2 rimmed baking sheets. Spread each with tomato sauce and top with cheese and other toppings of your choice.

Bake until the cheese has melted and the crust is crisp and golden, 10–15 minutes. Cut into wedges and serve.

Whether you're making mini pizzas for a party, or a large one for a family dinner, there are all kinds of possibilities when it comes to pizza. Try folding the dough over to make a gooey calzone, slicing the dough for cheesy breadsticks, or have fun experimenting with your favorite pizza toppings.

more pizza dough ideas

Moon pie Round mozzarella slices look like moons in a red sky. The melted rounds of cheese, paired with fresh basil and tomato sauce, make up the traditional Pizza Margherita, a classic kid favorite.

Calzone Sprinkle your favorite pizza ingredients over half of a dough round. Brush one edge with water, fold the dough over the ingredients, press to seal, then bake.

Cheese sticks Roll out the dough into a large rectangle, then cut it crosswise into 1-inch strips. Sprinkle with grated Parmesan and bake in a 425ºF oven for 15 minutes.

crispy chicken bites

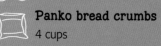

Vegetable oil cooking spray
for greasing

All-purpose flour
2 cups

Salt 2 teaspoons

Pepper ¼ teaspoon

Large eggs 2, whisked

Panko bread crumbs
4 cups

Boneless, skinless chicken breasts
4, cut into 1-inch strips

Honey 1 tablespoon

Brown sugar
1 tablespoon, firmly packed

Ketchup ⅓ cup

Mustard 2 tablespoons

Makes 4 servings

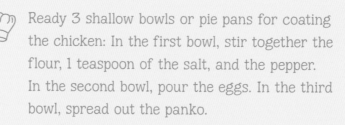

Preheat the oven to 450°F. Lightly grease a rimmed baking sheet with cooking spray.

Ready 3 shallow bowls or pie pans for coating the chicken: In the first bowl, stir together the flour, 1 teaspoon of the salt, and the pepper. In the second bowl, pour the eggs. In the third bowl, spread out the panko.

Working with 1 piece at a time, dip the chicken into the flour, coating it completely and shaking off the excess; then into the egg, allowing the excess to drip off; and finally into the panko, again shaking off the excess. Lay the coated chicken pieces on the prepared baking sheet.

Bake until crisp and golden brown, about 30 minutes.

Meanwhile, make the dipping sauce. In a bowl, whisk together the honey, brown sugar, ketchup, and mustard, and the remaining 1 teaspoon salt until mixed. Transfer to individual dipping bowls.

Serve the chicken hot from the oven with the sauce.

creamy corn chowder

Working with 1 ear of corn at a time and holding it upright with the stem end down, cut straight down between the cob and the kernels, freeing the kernels. Give the ear a quarter turn after each cut. Set the kernels aside, discarding the ears.

In a stockpot over medium heat, sauté the bacon until crisp, about 8 minutes.

 Add the corn, potatoes, celery, carrot, onion, broth, and cream to the pot and stir well.

Raise the heat to high and bring to a boil. Reduce the heat to medium-low and simmer, uncovered, until the vegetables are tender, about 20 minutes. Season to taste with salt and pepper.

Ladle the chowder into soup mugs and serve hot.

 Corn 4 ears

 Bacon 2 slices, diced

 Small boiling potatoes
5, peeled and diced

 Celery 2 stalks, diced

 Carrot 1, peeled and diced

 Yellow onion
½, diced

 Chicken broth
4 cups

 Heavy cream 1 cup

 Salt and pepper
to taste

Makes 6–8 mugs of chowder

homemade fish sticks with tartar sauce

 Frozen filo dough
4 sheets, thawed

 Butter 5 tablespoons, melted

 Halibut or cod fillets ½ pound, cut into 8 equal pieces

 Mayonnaise ½ cup

 Celery ¼ stalk, minced

 Pickle relish
2 tablespoons

 Lemon juice
1 tablespoon

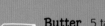 **Salt** ¼ teaspoon

Makes 8 fish sticks

Preheat the oven to 375°F. Line a rimmed baking sheet with parchment paper.

Lay 1 filo sheet on a clean work surface. Brush lightly with a little melted butter. Fold the filo in half lengthwise, and then cut in half crosswise. Cover the 2 filo pieces with a damp paper towel. Repeat with the remaining 3 sheets.

Working with 1 filo piece at a time, place it with a short end facing you, and brush it lightly with butter. Put a piece of fish on the bottom third of the filo, positioning it parallel to the bottom edge. Fold in the long sides and then roll up the filo to enclose the fish. Brush the seam lightly with butter to secure. Insert a wooden ice-pop stick into one end of the packet. Repeat to make 8 packets total.

Arrange the fish sticks, seam side down, on the prepared baking sheet.

Bake until golden brown, 15–20 minutes.

Meawhile, make the tartar sauce. In a bowl, whisk together the mayonnaise, celery, relish, lemon juice, and salt. Serve the tartar sauce alongside the fish sticks.

classic beef tacos

 Canola oil
1 tablespoon plus ¼ cup

 Yellow onion ¼ cup
chopped

 Garlic 1 clove, minced

 Ground beef 1 pound

 Ground cumin
1 teaspoon

 Sweet paprika
2 teaspoons

 Chili powder
2 teaspoons

 Salt and pepper
1 teaspoon each

 Corn tortillas 6
(6-inch)

 Lettuce ½ cup shredded

 Plum (roma)
tomatoes 2, diced

 Avocado 1, diced

Cheddar cheese
½ cup shredded

Makes 6 tacos

In a sauté pan over medium heat, warm the 1 tablespoon oil. Add the onion and garlic and sauté until softened, about 5 minutes. Add the ground beef and cook, stirring to break up the meat, until browned, 8–10 minutes. Drain and discard all but 1 tablespoon of the fat. Add the cumin, paprika, chili powder, salt, and pepper to the beef and stir until combined. Add ¼ cup water to the pan and bring to a simmer. Reduce the heat to low and let simmer, partially covered, until most of the water is absorbed, about 10 minutes. Remove from the heat and keep warm.

In another sauté pan over medium heat, warm the ¼ cup oil. Working with 1 tortilla at a time and using tongs, carefully slip the tortilla into the hot oil and cook, turning once, until lightly browned on both sides, about 3 minutes total. Transfer to paper towels to drain. Let cool slightly.

 When the tortillas are cool enough to handle, top each one with the beef mixture, dividing evenly. Then sprinkle each one with equal amounts of lettuce, tomatoes, avocado, and cheese.

Fold each taco in half and serve right away.

It's hard to go wrong with tortillas, spiced hamburger meat, beans, and cheese. And there are all kinds of different ways to use these yummy ingredients. You can roll them up in flour tortillas to make burritos, or sprinkle them onto tortilla chips along with lettuce and sour cream for bite-size tostadas.

more taco ideas

Seven-layer dip In a glass bowl, layer refried beans, taco meat, sour cream, shredded lettuce, Cheddar cheese, diced tomato, and cubed avocado. Use crisp tortilla chips for scooping down to the bottom.

Nachos Arrange tortilla chips on an ovenproof plate. Top with taco meat and plenty of shredded Monterey jack or Cheddar cheese. Broil until melted, then sprinkle with toppings like tomatoes and avocado.

Taco salad Fill a salad bowl with shredded lettuce. Top with taco meat, whole black beans, diced tomato and avocado, crushed tortilla chips, and fresh salsa.

chicken chow mein

 To make the sauce, in a liquid measuring cup, whisk together the soy sauce, ¼ cup water, rice vinegar, peanut oil, and cornstarch. Set aside.

Bring a large pot of water to a boil over high heat. Add the noodles and cook until al dente, about 5 minutes. Drain.

In a large sauté pan or wok over high heat, warm the oil. Add the chicken and cook, stirring, until browned, about 5 minutes. Remove from the pan and set aside.

Add the mushrooms, bok choy, baby corn, snap peas, and bean sprouts to the pan. Cook, stirring constantly, until softened, about 5 minutes. Drizzle the soy sauce mixture over the vegetables and cook, stirring, until the sauce has thickened, about 5 minutes. Return the cooked chicken to the pan, add the noodles, and toss to mix.

 Soy sauce ¼ cup

 Rice vinegar 2 teaspoons

 Peanut oil 1 teaspoon

 Cornstarch 1 teaspoon

 Fresh Chinese egg noodles 1 pound

 Canola oil 2 tablespoons

 Boneless, skinless chicken breasts 2, diced

 Small shiitake mushrooms ½ pound, halved

 Baby bok choy 3 heads, chopped

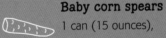 **Baby corn spears** 1 can (15 ounces), rinsed and drained

 Snap peas ½ pound

 Bean sprouts 1 cup

Makes 6 servings

spaghetti & meatballs

In a saucepan over medium heat, warm 2 tablespoons of the olive oil. Add the onion and garlic and sauté until the onion is soft, about 5 minutes. Add the tomato purée, chopped tomatoes, tomato paste, 1 tablespoon of the oregano, and the sugar. Bring to a simmer and cook until thickened, about 20 minutes.

 Meanwhile, make the meatballs. In a large bowl, combine the turkey, bread crumbs, Parmesan cheese, eggs, and the remaining 1 tablespoon oregano. Season with salt and pepper. Using clean hands, mix together. Scoop out tablespoon-sized portions of the mixture, rolling each one between your palms to make small balls.

In a large sauté pan, heat the remaining 1 tablespoon oil. Working in batches, add the meatballs and cook, turning as needed, until browned on all sides, about 8 minutes. Add the browned meatballs to the tomato sauce and simmer over low heat until the meatballs are cooked through, about 20 minutes.

While the meatballs simmer, bring a large pot of salted water to a boil over high heat. Add the spaghetti, stir well, and cook until al dente, about 8 minutes or according to the package directions. Drain and transfer to warmed serving bowls. Pour the sauce and meatballs over the top, toss gently, sprinkle with Parmesan, and serve.

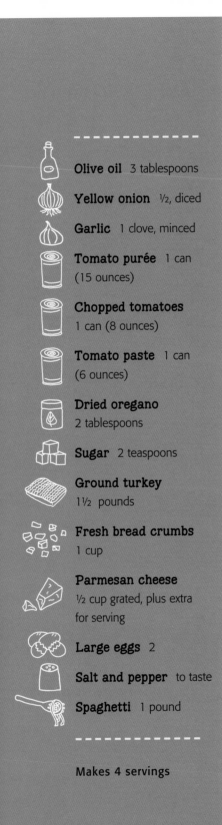

Olive oil 3 tablespoons

Yellow onion ½, diced

Garlic 1 clove, minced

Tomato purée 1 can (15 ounces)

Chopped tomatoes 1 can (8 ounces)

Tomato paste 1 can (6 ounces)

Dried oregano 2 tablespoons

Sugar 2 teaspoons

Ground turkey 1½ pounds

Fresh bread crumbs 1 cup

Parmesan cheese ½ cup grated, plus extra for serving

Large eggs 2

Salt and pepper to taste

Spaghetti 1 pound

Makes 4 servings

 Olive oil 3 tablespoons

 Chicken 1 pound, diced

 Yellow onion ½, chopped

 Carrots 2, chopped

 Small baking potatoes 2, peeled and diced

 Flour 3 tablespoons

 Chicken broth 4 cups

 Salt and pepper to taste

 Heavy cream ½ cup

 Frozen green peas 1 cup

 Frozen puff pastry 1 sheet, thawed

 Butter 2 tablespoons, melted

Makes 6 potpies

chicken potpies

Preheat the oven to 350°F. In a large pot over medium heat, warm 2 tablespoons of the oil. Add the chicken and cook, stirring, until browned on all sides. Transfer to a plate and set aside.

Add the remaining 1 tablespoon oil to the pan. Add the onion and cook until transluscent, about 4 minutes. Add the carrots and potatoes and cook, stirring frequently, until they begin to soften, 5–6 minutes. Add the flour and stir to coat the vegetables evenly. Add the chicken broth, bring to a boil, and cook until the vegetables are tender and the mixture has thickened, about 5 minutes. Season generously with salt and pepper. Stir in the cream, the reserved chicken, and the peas. Stir until just heated through. Set aside to cool.

Meanwhile, on a floured surface, roll out the puff pastry into a large rectangle. Using a 3-inch round biscuit or cookie cutter, cut out 6 rounds. Using a small cookie or biscuit cutter, cut out a hole in the top of each round.

Ladle the chicken mixture into six 1-cup ovenproof dishes. Top with the pastry rounds, pinching around the edge to secure. Brush the tops with the melted butter.

Bake the potpies until the crust is puffed and golden, 20–25 minutes. Let cool slightly before serving.

cheese ravioli with cherry tomatoes

Part-skim ricotta cheese 1 cup

Grated Parmesan cheese ¼ cup, plus extra for sprinkling

Basil leaves 2 large, finely chopped, plus extra for garnish

Salt ½ teaspoon

Cherry tomatoes 1 pint, halved

Olive oil 2 tablespoons

Wonton wrappers 24

Makes 4–6 servings

 In a small bowl, stir together the ricotta cheese, Parmesan cheese, basil, and salt. Set aside.

In a sauté pan over medium heat, combine the tomatoes and olive oil. Cook, stirring occasionally, just until the tomatoes begin to soften and break down, about 8 minutes. Meanwhile, bring a large pot of water to a boil over high heat.

 To make the ravioli, fill a small bowl with water and set aside for sealing the ravioli. Lay the wonton wrappers on a clean work surface. Scoop 1 teaspoon of the cheese filling onto half of each wrapper. Dip your fingertip into the water and gently rub along the outer edge of a wonton wrapper. Fold the wrapper in half and seal by gently pressing along the edge. Repeat to dampen, fold, and seal the remaining ravioli.

Carefully slip the ravioli into the boiling water and cook just until the wrappers are transparent, about 3 minutes. Using a slotted spoon, transfer the ravioli to individual serving bowls, dividing them equally. Top each serving with a spoonful of the tomatoes, sprinkle with the remaining Parmesan cheese and basil, and serve.

sweets

Considering the gooey frostings, chocolate dipping, cookie cutting, batter swirling, and multitude of sparkly sugary sprinkles, it's no wonder kids love making desserts. With all these deliciously sweet ingredients to choose from, it's nearly impossible to make a mistake. Keep recipes simple, encourage a little freedom of expression, and you'll create a cooking experience that your young ones will relish for many years to come.

inside-out apple crisp

Using an apple corer, core the apples and set aside.

In a small bowl, stir together the oats, brown sugar, cinnamon, salt, and nutmeg until well mixed. Sprinkle the butter over the oat mixture. Using your fingertips, rub the butter into the sugar-oat mixture until the mixture holds together in small chunks.

Stuff an equal amount of the oat mixture into the center of each apple. Stand the apples upright in a baking pan just large enough to hold them. Pour the apple juice into the bottom of the pan.

Bake until golden and tender when pierced with a knife, about 35 minutes. Transfer the apples to individual serving bowls and serve warm.

Baking apples, such as Fuji or Golden Delicious 4 large

 Old-fashioned rolled oats ½ cup

 Brown sugar ¾ cup, firmly packed

 Ground cinnamon 1 teaspoon

 Salt ¼ teaspoon

 Ground nutmeg ¼ teaspoon

 Butter ½ cup (1 stick), cut into small cubes

 Apple juice ½ cup

Makes 4 servings

 Butter ¾ cup
(1½ sticks)

 Semisweet chocolate
8 ounces, chopped

 Large eggs 4

 Vanilla extract
1 teaspoon

 Sugar 1 cup

 All-purpose flour
1 cup

 Salt ¼ teaspoon

 **Creamy peanut
butter** 6 tablespoons

 Chocolate chips
¾ cup

Makes about
16 brownies

chocolate–peanut butter brownies

Preheat the oven to 350°F. Line a 9-inch square baking pan with parchment paper.

Combine the butter and chocolate in a heatproof bowl and place over (not touching) barely simmering water in a saucepan. Heat, stirring frequently, until melted and smooth, about 5 minutes. Remove from the heat and let cool slightly.

Break the eggs into a bowl. Using an electric mixer on medium speed, beat the eggs until light in color, about 4 minutes. Beat in the vanilla and sugar until well combined, then gradually stir in the cooled chocolate until blended. Using a rubber spatula, fold in the flour and salt until evenly combined.

Scoop the chocolate mixture into the prepared baking pan and smooth the top. Using a tablespoon, drop 6 tablespoon-size dollops of peanut butter evenly over the top. Sprinkle with the chocolate chips.

Bake until a toothpick inserted into the center comes out clean, 25–30 minutes. Transfer to a wire rack and let cool completely. Cut into squares and serve.

strawberry puddings

Pour ¼ cup water into a small bowl, sprinkle with the gelatin, and stir to combine. Let stand for 5 minutes to soften.

In a saucepan over medium heat, stir together the milk, confectioners' sugar, and vanilla bean. Bring to a simmer for 5 minutes. Add the gelatin mixture and stir until dissolved. Remove from heat and let cool. When the milk mixture has cooled, remove the vanilla bean and discard.

Add the buttermilk and 1 cup of the diced strawberries to the milk mixture and stir together until combined.

Divide the strawberry mixture evenly among 4–6 small glasses, filling them to within about ½ inch of the rim. Cover and refrigerate the glasses and the remaining 1 cup strawberries until the puddings are set, at least 3 hours or up to 2 days.

Spoon the reserved chilled strawberries over the puddings and serve cold.

Powdered gelatin
3 teaspoons

Milk 1 cup

Confectioners' sugar
¾ cup

Vanilla bean 1, split

Buttermilk 2½ cups

Strawberries 2 cups,
hulled and diced

Makes 4–6 pudding
cups

Ingredients

 Granulated sugar
1½ cups

 Butter ¾ cup (1½ sticks)
plus 1 tablespoon, at room
temperature

 Large eggs 3

 Milk ¾ cup

 Vanilla extract
1 tablespoon plus
1 teaspoon

 All-purpose flour
2¾ cups

 Cornstarch
2 tablespoons

 Baking powder
1 tablespoon

 Salt ⅛ teaspoon

 Cream cheese 8 ounces

 Confectioners' sugar
2 cups

 Shredded coconut
2 cups

Makes 24 cupcakes

snowball cupcakes

Preheat the oven to 350°F.

 Line two 12-cup muffin pans with paper liners.
In a large bowl, using an electric mixer on medium
speed, beat together the granulated sugar and the
¾ cup butter until creamy. Add the eggs, one at
time, beating well after each addition. Add the
milk, ½ cup water, and the 1 tablespoon vanilla
and beat until combined.

 In a bowl, stir together the flour, cornstarch,
baking powder, and salt. With the mixer on low
speed, gradually add the flour mixture to the egg
mixture, beating until smooth. Divide the batter
among the prepared muffin cups, filling them
about two-thirds full.

Bake until a toothpick inserted in the center comes out clean,
35–40 minutes. Let cool on a wire rack for 5 minutes, then
remove the cupcakes from the pan and let cool completely.

To make the frosting, in a large bowl, whisk together the
cream cheese, the 1 tablespoon butter, and the 1 teaspoon
vanilla. Add the confectioners' sugar and stir until smooth.

 Generously frost each cupcake, sprinkle with the
shredded coconut, and eat!

Cupcakes are a classic party favorite and kids love to decorate their own. Set out plain cupcakes with bowls of icing and a range of toppings, and the celebration will swing into gear before the first one is finished. Make sure each child has two to decorate, one to enjoy at the party and one to show off at home.

more cupcake ideas

Decorations Cupcake decorating contests are a great way to get kids into the spirit of decorating. Try having a face-making contest, or encourage decorating with a theme such as flowers, bugs, cars, or zoo animals. The more theme-appropriate toppings and sprinkles you offer, the more excitement you will create.

Colored icings Adding a few drops of food coloring to plain white icing makes for more colorful fun. Try spooning two colors of icing onto a cupcake top and swirling them together. Or, frost the cupcake with one color and then drizzle with another color.

 All-purpose flour
2⅓ cups, plus more
for dusting

 Baking powder
¼ teaspoon

 Salt ⅛ teaspoon

 Butter 1 cup
(2 sticks), softened

 Sugar ⅔ cup

 Large egg 1

 Vanilla extract
1½ teaspoons

 **Confectioners'
sugar** 1 cup

 Lemon juice
1 tablespoon plus
1 teaspoon

 Food coloring
2–3 drops of your
favorite color

Makes about
12 cookie flowers

cookie flower pops

In a bowl, stir together the flour, baking powder, and salt.
Set aside. In a bowl, using an electric mixer on medium
speed, beat the butter and sugar until fluffy and light,
about 5 minutes. Add the egg and vanilla and beat until
well combined. With the mixer on low speed, gradually
add the flour mixture and beat just until blended.

 Press the dough into 2 flat disks, wrap in plastic
wrap, and refrigerate until firm, about 1 hour.

Preheat the oven to 350°F.

 On a lightly floured work surface, roll out
each dough disk into a ¼-inch-thick round.
Using flower-shaped cookie cutters, cut out
shapes and place on 2 rimmed baking sheets.
Insert a wooden ice-pop stick into each flower.

Bake until golden, 15–20 minutes. Let cool briefly on the
pan, then transfer to wire racks and let cool.

 To make the icing, in a small bowl, stir together
the confectioners' sugar, lemon juice, and food
coloring until smooth. Decorate the cooled
cookies with the icing and enjoy!

Sugar cookie dough easily plays host to a range of possibilities. You can sandwich cookies with fillings of melted chocolate, peanut butter, or jam. Use a small cookie cutter to create a window in the top cookie before baking, if you like. Or, try dipping plain or filled cookies in melted chocolate.

more cookie ideas

Ice cream sandwiches Set out your favorite ice cream at room temperature to soften. Spoon onto a cookie, sandwiching another cookie on top. Freeze until the ice cream is firm.

Jam thumbprints Roll dough into small balls. Using your thumb, make an impression in each of the balls and bake. Once cooled, fill each cookie with jam.

Chocolate-dipped cookies Using a double boiler, melt 8 ounces of semisweet chocolate. Once the cookies are cool, dip in the chocolate and let the chocolate set before serving.

lemony berry bars

 Butter ½ cup (1 stick), softened, plus more for greasing

 All-purpose flour 1 cup plus 4 tablespoons

 Confectioners' sugar ¼ cup

 Ice water 1 tablespoon

 Vanilla extract 1 teaspoon

 Salt ¾ teaspoon

 Raspberry or other berry jam ¾ cup

 Large eggs 6

 Granulated sugar 2 cups

 Lemon juice ¾ cup

Baking powder ¾ teaspoon

Makes about 16 bars

Preheat the oven to 350°F. Grease a 9-inch square pan.

To make the crust, in a bowl, using an electric mixer on medium speed, beat the butter until creamy. With the mixer on low speed, add the 1 cup flour, confectioners' sugar, ice water, vanilla, and ½ teaspoon of the salt and beat just until the mixture forms a ball.

 Using clean hands, scoop the dough into the prepared pan and press to form an even layer over the pan bottom. Refrigerate for 10 minutes.

Bake the crust until golden and firm, about 15 minutes. Let cool completely on a rack. Reduce the oven temperature to 325°F.

 Using a rubber spatula, spread the jam evenly over the crust. In a bowl, combine the eggs, granulated sugar, lemon juice, the 4 tablespoons flour, baking powder, and the remaining ¼ teaspoon salt. Whisk until smooth. Pour the egg mixture over the crust, spreading it with the back of the spatula to form an even layer.

Return the pan to the oven and bake until the top is set, 20–25 minutes. Let cool completely on a rack. Cut into bars or squares and serve.

 Frozen puff pastry
1 sheet, thawed

 **Pitted cherries or
blueberries** 2 cups

 Sugar 3 tablespoons

 Grated lemon zest
½ teaspoon

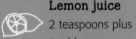 **Lemon juice**
2 teaspoons plus
1 tablespoon

 Ground cinnamon
⅛ teaspoon (optional)

 Large egg 1, lightly
beaten

 Confectioners' sugar
½ cup

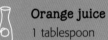 **Orange juice**
1 tablespoon

Makes 9 turnovers

fruity turnovers

Preheat the oven to 350°F. Line a baking sheet with parchment paper.

Place the pastry on a clean work surface. Using a rolling pin, roll out the pastry until it is a square that is ⅛-inch thick.

Cut the pastry lengthwise into 3 equal pieces, then cut the pieces crosswise to make a total of 9 squares. Place the squares on the prepared baking sheet and set aside.

In a bowl, combine the fruit, sugar, lemon zest, 2 teaspoons lemon juice, and cinnamon, if using. Divide the fruit mixture evenly among the pastry squares, placing it in the center of each square. Brush the edges of each square with the beaten egg. Fold the squares on the diagonal to enclose the filling, and press along the edge with a fork to seal in the filling.

Bake until golden brown, about 15 minutes. Transfer the turnovers to a rack to cool completely.

Meanwhile, make the glaze. In a bowl, whisk together the confectioners' sugar, orange juice, and remaining 1 tablespoon lemon juice. Drizzle the glaze over the cooled turnovers and serve.

ice cream bonbons

Line a baking sheet with waxed paper. Using a 2-inch ice cream scoop, scoop out 20 balls of ice cream, placing the balls on the prepared baking sheet. Have ready 20 small wooden cocktail picks.

 Poke a cocktail pick into each ice cream ball and place the baking sheet in the freezer until the balls are firm, 30–60 minutes. Meanwhile, set out several small bowls of your favorite topping ingredients.

Combine the chocolate and oil in a heatproof bowl and place over (not touching) barely simmering water in a saucepan. Heat, stirring frequently, until melted and smooth, about 5 minutes. Remove the bowl from the heat and let cool slightly.

 Dip the frozen ice cream balls into the melted chocolate, letting the excess drip back into the bowl, then dip into a topping ingredient. Place each bonbon back on the lined baking sheet. Return the pan to the freezer and freeze until the chocolate hardens, about 30 minutes. Serve the bonbons in a bowl, with the sticks up.

Favorite ice cream
1 pint

 Bonbon toppings
such as shredded
coconut and chopped
peanuts

 Dark chocolate
11 ounces, grated

 Canola oil
2 tablespoons

Makes 20 bonbons

The many uses for chocolate-covered ice cream balls is a topic most kids would love to explore. You can dip the bonbons into all kinds of toppings, from sprinkles to toasted nuts to candies. Let your imagination go wild, with more fanciful desserts like banana splits, bonbon kabobs, or a bonbon "cake."

more bonbon ideas

Banana split Nestle two bonbons between slices of fresh banana and a dollop of cherry-topped whipped cream. Use a spoon to break through the bonbons' hard chocolate shells, and enjoy!

Bonbon skewers Thread bonbons onto skewers, alternating them with fresh or frozen strawberries, raspberries, or banana slices.

Ice cream cake Arrange bonbons around the perimeter of your favorite cake as a decoration. When the cake is cut, everyone gets a bonbon or two with their slice for an instant cake and ice cream dessert.

waffle iron

An electric, countertop appliance used to make waffles. Comes in different sizes and shapes, like round, square, and Belgian.

griddle

A flat, rectangular cooking surface—ideal for pancakes or French toast—which can be used over one or two burners.

cookie cutter

Metal cutters—in all different shapes and sizes—tend to be the best as they hold their shape and cut through dough easily.

large grater/shredder

A metal kitchen tool that makes it easy to shred cheese or grate citrus zest.

small sieve

A mesh bowl, either fine or coarse, that is used for draining liquids or making dry ingredients smooth and powdery.

electric mixer

A handheld mixer with different speeds that quickly whips egg whites or beats batters and doughs.

whisk

A balloon-shaped tool used to whip together liquid ingredients and batters for even consistency.

ladle

A long-handled spoon with a deep bowl that is used to serve soups or stews.

wooden spoon

A long-handled wooden spoon is the best choice for stirring foods while they cook, as it will not scratch the pan.

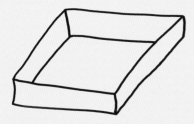

square pans

Metal baking pans, lined with parchment paper or aluminum foil, are great for baking brownies or bars.

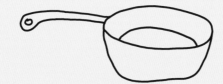

saucepans with lids

Deep pans that come in different sizes are used for stovetop cooking such as boiling pasta or simmering sauce.

frying pans

Shallow pans used on the stovetop for frying or cooking all kinds of food. The most common size is a 10-inch pan.

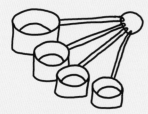

measuring cups

Straight-rimmed cups used for measuring dry ingredients. The straight sides make it easy to level off ingredients.

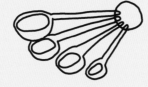

measuring spoons

A set of spoons, usually from ¼ teaspoon to 1 tablespoon, used to measure small amounts of dry or liquid ingredients.

liquid measuring cup

Cups used to measure liquids are clear glass so you can line up the amount of liquid with the correct marking on the side.

spatula

A wide, flat tool with thin edges that is used for slipping under food to flip or turn during cooking.

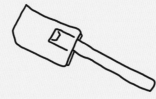

rubber spatula

A flexible rubber tool with a handle that is used to scrape the sides of mixing bowls and fold ingredients together.

rolling pin

A wooden or plastic tool used to roll out dough. Rolling pins with handles on each end are usually easier to use.

glossary

This list of common cooking terms and ingredients will help you when you are cooking the recipes in this cookbook.

bake
To cook items such as breads and pastries in an oven using hot, dry air.

baking powder
A white powder that is known as a chemical leavener which is used to make baked goods like breads and muffins rise. It is made up of baking soda, an acid such as cream of tartar, and cornstarch or flour. If your recipe calls for baking powder, you can substitute baking soda, an equal amount of cornstarch, and twice the amount of cream of tartar.

baking soda
Like baking powder, this is also a chemical leavener used to make baked goods rise. It is also known as bicarbonate of soda. Baking soda is commonly combined with an acidic ingredient like buttermilk or lemon juice to activate it. You cannot use baking powder as a replacement for baking soda.

beat
To mix ingredients vigorously with a spoon, fork, or the beaters on an electric mixer.

blend
To combine two or more ingredients thoroughly. Also, to mix ingredients in an electric blender.

boil
To heat a liquid until bubbles constantly rise to its surface and break. A gentle boil is when small bubbles rise and break slowly. A rapid boil is when large bubbles rise and break quickly.

buttermilk
A cultured milk, often lowfat, that has a thickened texture and tangy flavor. It is delicious in baked goods like biscuits.

chill
To place an item in the refrigerator until it is cold all the way through. Chilling helps to firm up or set some dishes, like puddings.

chocolate
Chocolate is available in many different forms, including semisweet chocolate: dark, sweet chocolate sold as blocks, bars, and chips; and unsweetened chocolate: solid chocolate that has no added milk or sugar which is sold in small squares and often used for baking. Unsweetened cocoa powder—which is not the same as hot cocoa mix—is a fine chocolate powder that is often used for baking.

chop
To cut food into evenly-sized pieces. Finely chopped pieces are small; coarsely chopped pieces are large.

cinnamon
A sweet, brown spice made from grinding the bark of the tropical evergreen tree.

coat
To cover the surface of a pan or baking dish or an ingredient like chicken with butter, oil, flour, crumbs, or another ingredient.

cobbler
A deep-dish fruit dessert topped with a biscuit topping, sprinkled with sugar, and baked until bubbly.

coconut (packaged)
A firm, white fruit that is available flaked or shredded, sweetened or unsweetened.

consistency
How thick or thin, fine or coarse, smooth or lumpy an ingredient or mixture of ingredients is.

cornmeal
Flour that is ground from dried corn kernels. It may be finely or coarsely ground. Stone-ground cornmeal is preferred by many home cooks because it contains the germ of the corn, giving it more texture and making it more flavorful and nutritious.

cream cheese
A soft, creamy, spreadable cheese made from cow's milk. It has a mildly tangy flavor and is often used in cheesecake.

cream, heavy
Cream is what rises to the top of milk. It's very rich and contains a lot of fat, up to 40 percent. Also called whipping cream, this is what you use to make whipped cream.

disk

A flat round shape. Dough is often formed into disks before rolling out and for easy storage in the refrigerator or freezer.

dissolve

To mix a fine-textured, solid ingredient, such as sugar or salt, into a liquid, such as water, until the solid disappears.

divide

To split ingredients or a batch of dough or batter into smaller, usually equal, quantities.

dollop

A heaping spoonful of an ingredient such as whipped cream or sour cream that is used to garnish food like soup, tacos, or pie.

drain

To pour off liquid, leaving the solids behind. To do this, the solids and liquid are usually poured into a strainer or colander.

drizzle

To pour an ingredient like icing or lemon juice over food in a thin stream.

dust

To cover a food, your hands, or a work surface lightly with a powdery substance such as flour or confectioners' sugar.

edamame

The Japanese name for green soy beans. Often served in their pods, sprinkled with salt. To eat, pop the beans out of the pod.

eggs

Sold in a range of sizes, from small to extra-large. The recipes in this book use large-sized eggs. Look for organic, free-range eggs for the best quality.

flour, all-purpose

The most common type of flour available, all-purpose is made from a blend of wheats that make it equally reliable for muffins, cakes, cookies, and other baked goods.

frosting

A sweet mixture similar to icing that is used to fill and top cakes, cupcakes, and cookies. It can be flavored with vanilla, chocolate, lemon, or other flavors.

garnish

To decorate a dish before serving. Also, the food used to decorate a dish. For example, you can garnish a bowl of soup with a dollop of sour cream or a sprinkle of fresh herbs.

gelatin

A thickener which helps puddings, molded desserts, marshmallows, and jellied candies keep their shape.

granola

A breakfast food or snack made from a mixture of grains, nuts, and dried fruits.

grate

To cut an ingredient, such as Parmesan, into very fine pieces on the surface of very small, sharp-edged holes on a grater/shredder.

grease

To rub a pan or baking dish with butter or oil to prevent sticking.

heat (stove)

A recipe should tell you the heat level to use on the stovetop. Heat levels are marked on the dial for each burner. Low heat is usually just above the lowest setting, which recipes sometimes call very low. Medium heat is when the dial is turned on halfway. High heat comes when the dial is at its highest setting. Medium-low and medium-high heats are midway between those two settings. Gas burners allow you to see the flame to help judge the heat level.

heatproof

Dishes that can be used in the oven or on top of a stove.

hummus

A spread made from chickpeas, tahini, lemon juice, garlic, and olive oil.

invert

To turn a pan upside down so that the food falls gently onto a cooling rack or a dish.

jam

A sweet, chunky preserve containing the edible portion of the fruit in its entirety.

jelly roll

A thin sheet of cake layered with jelly and then rolled up. A jelly roll pan refers to a rimmed cookie sheet or sheet pan.

kabob

Pieces of meat, vegetables, or fruits served on a wooden or metal skewer. Meats and vegetables are often marinated and grilled.

knead

To work a yeasted dough with your hands or a mixer, using pressing, folding, and turning motions. When dough is fully kneaded, it becomes smooth and elastic.

lengthwise

In the same direction as, or parallel to, the longest side of a piece of food or a pan or dish. This term is often used in directions for serving or cutting.

line

To cover the inside of a pan with aluminum foil, waxed paper, or parchment paper to prevent food from sticking.

maple syrup

Pure maple syrup is made from the boiled sap of the sugar maple tree. For the best flavor look for pure maple syrup rather than what's known as "pancake syrup," which is often made from corn syrup.

melt

To heat a solid substance, such as butter or chocolate, just until it becomes liquid.

mix

To stir together dry or wet ingredients until they are combined.

mound

To heap ingredients into a raised mass.

muffin

A cup-shaped quick bread that can either be savory, such as cornmeal, or sweet, such as blueberry or chocolate.

nutmeg

The hard seed of the nutmeg tree. This fragrant spice is grated or ground and most often used in desserts like pumpkin pie.

panko

Dried, Japanese-style bread crumbs, which cook up extra crispy when used to coat ingredients like chicken or shrimp.

peanut butter

Made from ground peanuts, this spreadable "butter" is used for sandwiches and more.

peel

To strip or cut away the skin or rind from fruits and vegetables.

pinch

The amount of a dry ingredient that you can pick up, or "pinch," between your thumb and forefinger; usually less than about ⅛ teaspoon. Often used to measure salt, pepper, and heavy spices.

popover

A very light, hollow, eggy muffin that puffs up when it is baked.

preheat

To heat an oven to a specific temperature before using it.

puff pastry

A light, flaky pastry that is formed by rolling and folding dough and butter in many layers so that it expands when it is baked.

raisins

Sweet, dried grapes that are used in a variety of baked products.

reduce (heat)

To turn down the heat under a pan on the stovetop or inside the oven.

refrigerate

To place food in the refrigerator to chill, to become firm, or for storage.

rise

What happens to a dough or batter when it becomes bigger and more airy as a result of the gas (carbon dioxide) released by yeast, baking powder, or baking soda.

roll out

To flatten dough with a rolling pin until it is smooth, even, and typically thin.

room temperature

The temperature of a comfortable room. Butter or eggs are often brought to room temperature so they will blend more easily into a batter or dough.

set

When a liquid congeals and thickens or when a dough or batter becomes more solid as it cooks or cools.

set aside

To put ingredients to one side while you do something else.

shortening, vegetable

A solid fat made from vegetable oil and used in cooking and baking.

shred

To cut an ingredient, such as carrots or cheese, on the medium or large holes of a grater/shredder.

simmer

To cook something slowly on the stovetop at just below the boiling point. The surface should be steaming and nearly bubbling.

slice

To cut food lengthwise or crosswise with a knife, forming thick or thin pieces.

soften

To let an ingredient, such as butter, sit at room temperature until it is soft enough to spread or mix.

spread

To apply a soft food, such as frosting or butter, over another food in an even layer.

stir

To move a spoon, fork, whisk, or other utensil continuously—usually in a circular motion—through dry or wet ingredients to combine them.

sugar

The three most common sugars are: granulated sugar (small, white granules), brown sugar (a moist blend of granulated sugar and molasses), and confectioners' sugar (finely ground granulated sugar with a small amount of cornstarch).

tartar sauce

A creamy, tangy sauce that is usually made from mayonnaise, capers, chopped dill pickles or pickle relish, lemon, and herbs. Often served with fish or shellfish.

thicken

When a food changes from a loose, liquid consistency to a thick, firm one.

tortillas, whole wheat

Flatbreads that are cooked on a griddle and made from wheat flour. They are used in Mexican cooking and can be eaten plain or wrapped around fillings such as beans, rice, and/or grilled meats and poultry.

toss

To mix ingredients together by tumbling them in the bowl with your hands, two forks, or two spoons.

vanilla extract

A liquid flavoring made from vanilla beans, the dried pods of a type of orchid. Look for pure vanilla extract for better flavor.

whisk

To stir a liquid such as heavy cream or egg whites vigorously with a whisk, adding air and increasing its volume until fluffy.

work surface

A clean, flat space—usually in the kitchen—used for cutting, mixing, or preparing foods.

yeast, quick-rise or rapid-rise

A microscopic organism that makes breads rise. In recent years, quick-rise yeasts have been developed to make breads rise in only half the usual time.

yogurt

A custardlike, cultured milk product that has a tangy flavor, and can be plain or sweetened and flavored with fruit.

zest

The thin, brightly colored outer layer of peel of a citrus fruit. It is most often grated or cut into strips.

index

weldonowen

415 Jackson Street, Suite 200, San Francisco, CA 94111

www.weldonowen.com

LITTLE COOKS

Conceived and produced by Weldon Owen Inc.

Copyright © 2009 Weldon Owen Inc. and Williams-Sonoma, Inc.

This book has been previously published as
Williams-Sonoma Cooking Together

This edition first printed in 2013

10 9 8 7 6 5 4 3 2 1

Library of Congress Cataloging-in-Publication
Data is available.

ISBN-13: 978-1-61628-544-9

ISBN-10: 1-61628-544-3

Printed in China by Toppan-Leefung

ACKNOWLEDGMENTS

Weldon Owen would like to thank the following individuals
for their generous assistance in making this book a reality:
Text Writer Lisa Atwood, Photographer David Matheson,
Food Stylist Erin Quon, Prop Stylist Lauren Hunter,
Digital Technicians Eszter Marosszeky & William Moran,
Assistant Food Stylist Victoria Woollard, as well as Ken DellaPenta,
Leslie Evans, and Sharon Silva. A special thanks to homeowners
Lauren and Brad Hancock and models Sam Blake, Sean O'Neal,
Teya O'Neal, Erin Quon, Tatum Quon, Clara Tunny, Mia Turner,
and Ozzy Wilson